FORREST GRIFFIN

By John Hamilton

Published by ABDO Publishing Company, 8000 West 78th Street, Suite 310, Edina, MN 55439. Copyright ©2011 by Abdo Consulting Group, Inc. International copyrights reserved in all countries. No part of this book may be reproduced in any form without written permission from the publisher. A&D Xtreme™ is a trademark and logo of ABDO Publishing Company.

Printed in the United States of America, North Mankato, Minnesota.
052010
092010

 PRINTED ON RECYCLED PAPER

Editor: Sue Hamilton
Graphic Design: John Hamilton
Cover Photo: AP Images
Interior Photos: Ray Kasprowicz, p. 1, 12, 12-13, 20-21, 26-27, 28-29, 29;
AP Images, p. 6-7, 8-9, 10, 11, 14-15, 16, 16-17, 18-19, 21, 22-23, 24-25, 30-31;
Getty Images, p. 4-5, 25, 32.

Library of Congress Cataloging-in-Publication Data

Hamilton, John, 1959-
  Forrest Griffin / John Hamilton.
     p. cm. -- (Xtreme UFC)
  Includes index.
  ISBN 978-1-61613-475-4
  1. Griffin, Forrest--Juvenile literature. 2. Martial artists--United States--Biography--Juvenile literature. I. Title.
  GV1113.G75H36 2011
  796.8092--dc22
  [B]
                                  2010016174

CONTENTS

FORREST

Forrest Griffin is one of the most popular fighters in mixed martial arts. He is a former Ultimate Fighting Championship (UFC) light heavyweight champion. He continues to thrill fans with his scrappy fighting style.

GRIFFIN

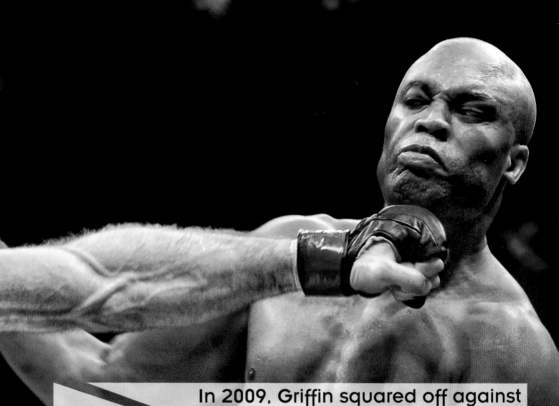

In 2009, Griffin squared off against Anderson Silva. He lost the fight, but came back later that year more determined than ever to show he is a true champion.

Xtreme Fight

UFC.COM

FIGHTER

Name: Forrest Griffin

Born: March 16, 1979, Columbus, Ohio

Height: 6 feet, 3 inches (1.9 m)

Weight: 205 pounds (93 kg)

Nationality: American

Division: Light Heavyweight—186 to 205 pounds (84 to 93 kg)

Reach: 77 inches (196 cm)

Fighting Style: Brazilian jiu-jitsu, kickboxing

Fighting Out Of: Las Vegas, Nevada

Martial Arts Rank: Brown belt in Brazilian jiu-jitsu

Mixed Martial Arts Record (as of April 2010)

> **Total Fights:** 23
>
> **Wins:** 17 (3 by knockout, 7 by submission, 7 by decision)
>
> **Losses:** 6

STATS

Forrest Griffin's UFC Fight Record (including The Ultimate Fighter 1)

Event	Date	Result	Opponent	Method
UFC 106	11/21/2009	Win	Tito Ortiz	Split Decision
UFC 101	8/8/2009	Loss	Anderson Silva	Knock Out
UFC 92	12/27/2008	Loss	Rashad Evans	Technical Knockout
UFC 86	7/5/2008	Win	Quinton Jackson	Unanimous Decision
UFC 76	9/22/2007	Win	Mauricio Rua	Submission
UFC 72	1/16/2007	Win	Hector Ramirez	Unanimous Decision
UFC 66	12/30/2006	Loss	Keith Jardine	Technical Knockout
UFC 62	8/26/2006	Win	Stephan Bonnar	Unanimous Decision
UFC 59	4/15/2006	Loss	Tito Ortiz	Split Decision
UFC 55	10/7/2005	Win	Elvis Sinosic	Technical Knockout
UFC 53	6/4/2005	Win	Bill Mahood	Submission
TUF 1	4/9/2005	Win	Stephan Bonnar	Unanimous Decision

UFC = Ultimate Fighting Championship
TUF = *The Ultimate Fighter*

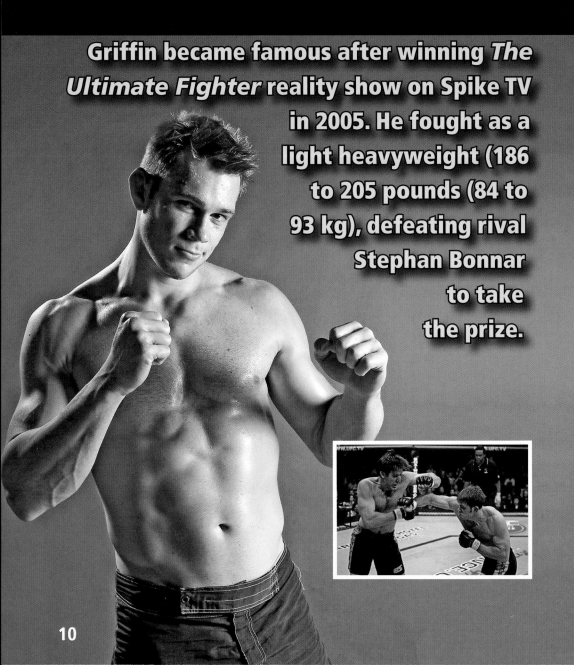

EARLY

Griffin became famous after winning *The Ultimate Fighter* reality show on Spike TV in 2005. He fought as a light heavyweight (186 to 205 pounds (84 to 93 kg), defeating rival Stephan Bonnar to take the prize.

CAREER

At UFC 76 in 2007, Griffin battled Mauricio "Shogun" Rua, defeating the heavily favored Brazilian fighter in three rounds of hard-hitting action.

FIGHT

TRAINING

As a former police officer from Augusta, Georgia, Griffin believes in hard work and willpower. His tough workouts prepare him both physically and mentally.

HIGHLIGHTS

Xtreme Fight

At UFC 86, on July 5, 2007, Griffin fought rival *Ultimate Fighter* coach Quinton "Rampage" Jackson. The underdog Griffin won a unanimous decision after five rounds.

UFC 86 Vs. Rampage Jackson

Both Griffin and Jackson scored damaging kicks and punches. In the first round, Jackson scored with a big uppercut. But Griffin came back with powerful leg kicks and punches in round two. After five full rounds of exciting action, Griffin was declared the UFC light heavyweight champion.

UFC 92 Vs. Rashad Evans

On December 27, 2008, Griffin stepped into the Octagon with undefeated challenger Rashad Evans. With the light heavyweight title on the line, Griffin controlled the first two rounds with his aggressive kickboxing style.

Taken Down

In round three, Griffin continued scoring with punches and kicks. But Evans finally caught Griffin's leg and took him to the ground. Shortly afterward, Evans executed a painful flurry of ground and pound. The referee stopped the fight, with Griffin losing by TKO (technical knockout).

UFC 101 Vs. Anderson Silva

In Griffin's return to the Octagon on August 8, 2009, he squared off against Brazilian jiu-jitsu fighter Anderson Silva. As the fight began, the scrappy Griffin was clearly the crowd favorite. But Silva would soon show why he is considered one of the best pound-for-pound fighters in UFC history.

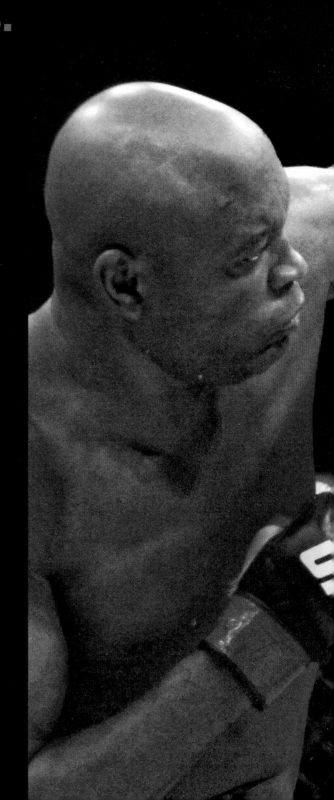

Tough Loss

Just three minutes and 23 seconds into round one, Silva knocked Griffin to the canvas with a precision jab. Griffin took the loss hard. Some fans thought his career might be over. Could the defeated Griffin make a comeback?

UFC 106 Vs. Tito Ortiz

On November 21, 2009, Griffin fought a rematch against Tito Ortiz, the legendary UFC star known as the Huntington Beach Bad Boy. During their first match in 2006, Griffin lost to Ortiz's superior wrestling and boxing skills. This time, Griffin was determined to kick and punch his way to victory.

Comeback Kid

Griffin showed superior striking skills against Ortiz. It was a major improvement over their first match. After three full rounds, Griffin won the decision. He proved to himself and fans that with hard work and determination, he still had what it takes to be a UFC champion.

Brazilian Jiu-Jitsu

A fighting style made popular by fighters from Brazil that specializes in grappling and ground fighting, including chokes and joint locks.

Decision

If a match finishes without a clear winner, either by knockout or submission, a panel of three judges determines the victor. If only two judges agree on the winner, it is called a split decision.

Ground and Pound

A style of fighting where an opponent is taken down and then punched or submitted.

Jab

A strike used in boxing and karate. When in a fighting stance, the lead fist is thrown straight out. Jabs are not as powerful as regular punches, but they are very quick and effective.

GLOSSARY

Kickboxing
A style of fighting that relies mainly on a mix of kicking and punching. Muay Thai is a type of kickboxing that is the national sport of Thailand.

Mixed Martial Arts
A full-contact sport that allows a mix of different martial arts, such as boxing, karate, and wrestling. The most popular mixed martial arts (MMA) organization is the Ultimate Fighting Championship (UFC).

Octagon
The eight-sided ring in which Ultimate Fighting Championship fighters compete.

Uppercut
A strike used in boxing and karate that starts low and sweeps upward, often connecting with an opponent's chin. It is often a match-ending strike.

INDEX